COVE COV

Bible St

7 Sessions for Homegroup
and Personal Use

Ecclesiastes

Hard questions and spiritual answers

Christopher Brearley

CWR

Contents

Introduction

A reader of Ecclesiastes may wonder why it is in the Bible. A casual glance gives the impression that the emphasis is upon fate rather than faith; upon happiness rather than holiness; upon the material rather than the spiritual; and upon this world rather than the next. Consequently, it is considered by many to be depressing rather than inspiring, for they fail to discover its relevance. The German poet, satirist and journalist Heinrich Heine called it the 'Song of Scepticism' (*Das Hohelied der Skepsis*). Some even regard it as a confession of failure, and claim that it serves no useful purpose. Nothing could be further from the truth:

By teaching with great emphasis in the first part of the book the meaninglessness of earthly things, the writer disillusions his readers. "'Meaningless! Meaningless!" says the Teacher, "Utterly meaningless! Everything is meaningless."' Does this reveal that the author is sceptical or troubled by doubt? Or is he inspired by God and giving words of comfort, guidance and a warning against placing confidence in the things of this world?

The word 'meaningless', sometimes translated 'vanity', appears many times in the book and could suggest an extremely pessimistic outlook upon life. This would be a mistake, for the original Hebrew word, 'hebel', means a 'vapour or breath', something that immediately condenses and disappears. Hence, the emphasis should be placed upon the transitory nature of earthly things. These soon pass away, and offer little while one has them.

Our life on earth is undoubtedly short in comparison to the overall picture. Probably most people reach a physical peak between the ages of 25 and 30 and then deteriorate. The older you get the more rapid the deterioration until eventually you die. This is a very depressing prospect if all that one can look forward to is extinction. One may have had a life of pleasure and maybe achieved great things, but is it worthwhile if physical and mental deterioration followed by death are the only certainties confronting us all? Or are they? Is everything meaningless?

Basic questions relating to life should always begin by asking 'why?' rather than 'how?'. People often ask how they can achieve happiness, do this or that, when they should be asking 'why?'. Science can attempt to tell us how the world began, but it can never tell us who created it and why. For that you need to read the Bible which clearly states that God made the world (Gen. 1:1); and the reason why, was for His own glory (Isa. 43:7). To believe these things you need faith, for they cannot be proved or refuted by intellectual deduction.

The major question that everyone needs to ask is whether or not life is worth living. What does one have to show for it at the end? Unfortunately only a few ever ask this question. Often people are so busy that they do not have time to stop and think about anything important. Some don't even want to think because they have no wish to confront the problems of life and death. They would accept the old adage that ignorance is bliss, but such a philosophy is questionable. A proverb says, 'Not to know is bad, not to wish to know is worse.' This is sound teaching, for running away from a situation by evading facts is never a positive way forward.

The aim of the writer of Ecclesiastes is to encourage us to use our eyes and our ears to observe and question the purpose of life. Does this include God? He makes no immediate rush to answer this question, and so he starts with the observable world. Therefore, not surprisingly, his initial analysis of life is depressing. One could easily presume that he was a deep thinker struggling with many problems, who finally arrives at unsatisfactory conclusions. However, careful observation clearly indicates that he's a man of God who writes with certainty about the future. He drops hints of this throughout, beginning with the vital phrase, 'under the sun'. This is reiterated almost 30 times by an author who does not waste words.

The following pages contain a series of studies that challenge the reader about the great questions of life. Irrelevant controversial issues have been avoided, including the authorship of Ecclesiastes. Although it is widely accepted by scholars that the writer was Solomon, it cannot be proved. This indicates that the human author is not important, while the message, which deals with practical matters and everyday life, is.

Obviously time does not stand still; the conditions of life are different from one generation to the next; but human nature remains always the same. There is nothing new under the sun. It has all been done before. What can you point to that is new? Hence, the advice of Ecclesiastes is relevant to every generation and so should be accepted with enthusiasm. It provides an effective guide to life and how it can be lived to the full. Ecclesiastes speaks for today.

Are you ready for the first session of the study? Let me suggest that you begin by reading all of Ecclesiastes at one sitting – there are only 12 short chapters. Then enjoy the search and may it end in the satisfaction which arises from fearing God and keeping His commandments. This is the duty of every person.

WEEK 1

Getting Nowhere

Opening Icebreaker

Discuss the routine of a typical day in your life. If you could change something, what would it be?

Bible Readings

- Ecclesiastes 1:3–9
- Matthew 16:26

Opening Our Eyes

Life can give the impression that everything is rushing in circles and getting nowhere. It can be likened to a treadmill; it goes round in a continual cycle and the result is that you finish where you started. The faster you run, the faster it goes, and whatever the speed it always ends in the same place. Similarly generations come and generations go, but the human condition and the underlying issues of the soul remain the same. Despite the perpetual change there is nothing new.

There is a regular consistency and continuity about nature, and the writer of Ecclesiastes provides three examples, starting with the sun. It rises and sets and repeats this process day after day, ever returning on its course. His other two examples are the wind and water. The only consistent thing about the wind is its changing direction, but it cannot blow in any direction in which it has not blown before. It continually veers or backs from point to point. Similarly streams of water unite with others on their onward flow, widening and deepening until they reach the sea, yet the sea is never full. Water is constantly taken up into the sky by evaporation to form clouds and then returns in the form of rain to the place of its origin. This repetitive circularity of nature can become very wearisome.

Like the sea, our senses are repeatedly fed, but never filled. There is always an insatiable appetite for variety and for something new. Adults frequently behave like children, ever eager for a new toy, but when they have played with it for a short while, they grow weary of it and must have another. It's very easy to become tired of seeing and hearing the same things and so there's a continual search for something different and better. The package tour industry is constantly trying to tempt us with new destinations. The fashion industry tries to tempt us with new designs. People are constantly striving for something new so as to attain satisfaction. But there is nothing new under the sun, for history repeats itself. Obviously there is progress or regression, but human nature is the same in every generation. What has been will be again, what has been done will be done again. Material things alone have never ultimately satisfied or solved the basic problems of life, and never will.

Mid-life crisis

Reference is sometimes made to the so-called 'mid-life crisis'. People realise that their life is probably past the halfway stage and this concentrates their minds upon the future. They may believe that they have achieved very little, if anything, in life. This coupled with the realisation that one is past the point of starting again can be very distressing. The monotonous routine of work can be likened to a treadmill and one can feel trapped with the choices one has made for one's lifestyle. What do people get for all their hard work? Certainly life can be very wearisome because everything can appear to be repetitious and meaningless.

Oscar Wilde's alleged comment that 'There are two kinds of tragedies in life: not getting what one wants, and getting what one wants' is true. The failure to attain a goal in life and to realise that it will never be achieved can result in great despondency and dissatisfaction. However, it is equally true that success does not necessarily satisfy. One may reach a peak only to discover that there's nothing there.

Discussion Starters

1. The writer of Ecclesiastes was a great observer of life. What characteristics are necessary to be observant?

2. What does one achieve by a lifetime of hard labour, if there is nothing beyond this life? Does one achieve anything, or is it all meaningless?

3. Does everything in life appear to be weary and tiresome?

4. What is the purpose of life, and am I getting anywhere? Am I satisfied and content, or concerned about the future?

5. Why do some suffer from the so-called 'mid-life crisis'?

_____

_____

_____

_____

6. Why are people forever looking for something new?

_____

_____

_____

_____

7. Is there anything of which one can say, 'Look! This is something new'?

_____

_____

_____

_____

8. Can one find true happiness without God?

_____

_____

_____

_____

Personal Application

The nineteenth-century preacher and author, Charles Bridges, succinctly says, 'Apart from God, the world is poor indeed. Disappointment brings weariness. Success gives no satisfaction.' Is life worth living? The answer to this question depends upon whether God is included or excluded. If you consider only earthly values all your activity and that of nature will appear to be futile. With God everything takes on a different perspective and what appears meaningless becomes meaningful. Are you living life to the full?

Seeing Jesus in the Scriptures

The teaching of Jesus clearly shows that it is useless for a person to gain the whole world, if they forfeit their soul (Matt. 16:26). Common sense should tell us that material things alone can never satisfy our deepest needs and that a constant striving for something new will become very wearisome.

The answer to this problem can be found in Jesus, who said, 'Come to me, all you who are weary and burdened, and I will give you rest' (Matt. 11:28). This is as relevant today as it was then and applies to anyone who tries to find fulfilment in life by their own exertion.

WEEK 2

The Search for Satisfaction

Opening Icebreaker

Imagine that you could have anything your eyes desired; what would it be? Give reasons for your choice.

Health, Happy and contented.

Bible Readings

- Ecclesiastes 1:12–2:26
- Ecclesiastes 5:19–20

Opening Our Eyes

Within life there are four major routes that can be tried to achieve satisfaction: education, enjoyment, employment and enrichment. The writer of Ecclesiastes was a great observer of life who tried all of these without success, as do many people today.

Because history repeats itself one would assume that it is important to learn from the experience of others. Unfortunately the German philosopher Georg Wilhelm Hegel was right when he said, 'What experience and history teach us is this – that people and governments never have learnt anything from history, or acted on principles deduced from it.' People today do the same things and reach the same conclusions as those of previous generations. There are many who learn by costly mistakes in the school of experience, whose colours are black and blue.

The routes toward satisfaction

Education: Some aim to achieve an academic goal. Their life can be completely dominated by the desire to accumulate knowledge but, though this may be stimulating, it can never provide complete satisfaction. A student will inevitably reach a point of disillusionment because the more they know, the more they realise their ignorance. In reality people know very little about anything.

Some believe that education can answer all problems; this idea is nothing new. In 1860 the English philosopher Jeremy Bentham said, 'If we can get universal and compulsory education by the end of the century, all our social, political and moral problems will be solved.' How mistaken he was! There are problems which human ingenuity can never solve. Only wisdom is adequate, and that is obtained not by natural education but by supernatural revelation.

Although it is desirable to be educated, the route of education will always fail to produce lasting contentment. At the end of life it is of no use, it dies with you. Ecclesiastes shows that to live for knowledge alone does not result in real life.

Enjoyment: We turn to the emotional, to the company of playboys. This man denied himself nothing his eyes desired (Eccl. 2:1–3). Notice that his mind still guided him with wisdom. He did not become a slave to these things, as many people do, for he knew that would only result in greater misery. It was a carefully conducted and controlled experiment to ascertain the value of various pleasures. Unfortunately there are many today who are seeking happiness through drink, drugs, gambling or sex, and they are usually miserable because of rejection, loneliness and fear. Eat, drink and be merry for tomorrow you die, is for some the complete philosophy of life. This is a mistake, for experience indicates that indulging in pleasures, whether crude or cultural, will not ultimately satisfy.

Employment: Many seek to find satisfaction and fulfilment through their pursuit of a career and their labours. This was clearly the experience of the writer of Ecclesiastes (2:10–11, 17–18, 22–23).

Enrichment: This final route is to invest in something that will last after death. It's the joy of creativity. One might undertake great projects like building houses, or making beautiful gardens (Eccl. 2:4–5). However, this also fails to satisfy. First, there is the realisation that it has all been done before. A second aggravation is that one must leave it all behind, for death is the great leveller (1 Tim. 6:7). This creates the problem that someone else inherits it, and who knows whether they will be a wise person or a fool (Eccl. 2:18–19).

Discussion Starters

1. We live in a world where the vast majority of people are dissatisfied. Despondency, disillusionment, depression and despair are common. Do you agree? If so, give your reasons.

2. The selfish and shallow joys of materialism and the acquisitive society are generally regarded to be the pathway to happiness. Does a brief, truthful reflection reveal the fallacy of this philosophy?

3. Is it true that lasting contentment is not derived from possessions, but from activities where self-advancement is not the primary motive?

4. The Earl of Shaftesbury in his nineteenth-century education campaign said, 'Education without instruction in religious and moral principles will merely result in a race of clever devils.' Discuss this statement.

5. The world attaches great significance to intellect, learning and understanding. Is this commendable?

_____

_____

_____

6. What is your major aim in life and why?

_____

_____

_____

7. Can anyone achieve happiness by constantly entertaining themselves? Read Psalm 16:8–9 and Galatians 5:22. Gladness and joy are based on God's presence within us. Can you relate this to your own life?

_____

_____

_____

8. Why do people become slaves to drink, drugs, gambling or sex? What can be done to help?

_____

_____

_____

Personal Application

The cost of the search can be frightful and lead to cynicism and despair because of the meaninglessness, the emptiness and the vanity of it all. The writer of Ecclesiastes repeatedly likens it to chasing after the wind, which is a purposeless occupation. It is to grasp at something and catch nothing.

Even so, these various routes – education, entertainment, employment and enrichment – can be meaningful and enjoyable. The person who believes in God is not necessarily someone who denies themselves the pleasures of life, but someone who desires that whatever they do will be to the glory of God. Only then does the meaningless become meaningful.

Seeing Jesus in the Scriptures

Whatever route you try in your search for satisfaction, there is only one way to God. Jesus said, 'I am the way and the truth and the life. No-one comes to the Father except through me' (John 14:6). Observe the pronoun 'I'. We are saved not by a principle but a Person. Christ is God, and only by faith in Him can you be forgiven your sins and one day reign with Him in glory.

WEEK 3

A Time for Everything

Opening Icebreaker

Discuss past major events that have changed the world for better or worse.

Bible Readings

- Ecclesiastes 3:1–11
- Haggai 1
- Luke 12:16–22
- Mark 13:32–37

Opening Our Eyes

Time is an extremely precious commodity because it is short, and what we do with it determines the kind of people that we become and the future that we have. Hence, time needs to be handled with the greatest respect, for a brief moment is sufficient to bring tremendous change to our lives. An accident, good fortune, illness, the loss of a loved one and so much more can suddenly transform our situation.

Within Ecclesiastes 3 there are 14 contrasting pairs of examples relating to time, which cover various aspects of life. Clearly they illustrate the ebb and flow of human experience and that there is a time for everything. Although life is full of contrasts – times when we are happy and times when we are sad – it also displays continuity. Everything in life follows a pattern. Night is followed by day, and winter followed by spring, and so the circle continues. Why should this happen? Is it because of chance or choice?

Many people believe that whatever happens in life is simply a matter of luck. There are some who believe that they can improve the situation by the possession of lucky charms, an attitude which the Bible condemns. Those who believe in God should not talk about luck because they do not believe that life is controlled by impersonal forces.

The alternative to chance is choice. There are some who claim that it is their choice and that they can do anything they want. Then there are those who believe that their fate is determined by others. Hence, they have someone to blame when things go wrong. Those in positions of responsibility are common targets for criticism.

Who is it that causes the seasons for every activity? The Bible says that God is in control but that individuals have a degree of liberty. Imagine that it's winter. You may decide to stay in a warm house or venture out into the cold. The choice is yours; what is predestined is that winter comes. God is sovereign, He sets the times, but you are responsible to use your time effectively, for once lost it cannot be reclaimed.

The purpose of life

The writer of Ecclesiastes reaches certain conclusions. He says that God gives us times of gladness and times of sadness. Consequently we are never guaranteed lives which are free from suffering. Quite the contrary! *Everyone* who wants to live a godly life will be persecuted (see 2 Tim. 3:12). However, even in times of difficulty it should be possible to praise God because 'He has made everything beautiful in its time' (Eccl. 3:11). There are times when it is difficult to understand why God allows things like severe suffering to happen. Life can be very cruel. Why do the wicked often prosper while the righteous suffer? To answer such questions it is necessary to try and see things from God's point of view and therefore you need a big concept of space and time. If your way of thinking is confined to this life only, then what happens will appear to be unjust. But if you have a longer-term view it's a completely different picture.

Paul, who suffered more than most, said, 'I consider that our present sufferings are not worth comparing with the glory that will be revealed in us' (Rom. 8:18). The severest suffering and trials for the Christian are nothing compared with the eternal glory that is to come.

Discussion Starters

1. What lessons relating to time can be learnt from Haggai 1?

2. The easiest answer when confronted with the needs of God's work is to say, 'Some other time.' Is there a danger that the time will never be right and the necessary work will not be done?

3. Discuss the demands made on your time. What determines how you use your time?

4. Can one ever justify being too busy to regularly read the Bible? Too busy to praise and to pray?

5. As soon as you are born you begin to die and before it's realised your time can be gone. How does the preciousness of time influence your way of thinking?

_____

_____

_____

_____

6. If one believes in a God of love, why is life so unfair? Why do the righteous often suffer while the wicked may prosper? Why doesn't God intervene? Why the delay? Surely it's not fair?

_____

_____

_____

_____

7. Discuss Mark 13:32–37. Why must one be alert at all times?

_____

_____

_____

_____

8. Does your response to God's calendar determine whether you find purpose in life?

_____

_____

_____

_____

Personal Application

It is not possible for people to see the whole scope of God's work from beginning to end. This is well illustrated in the life of Job who never knew the reason why he suffered; but he reached a point where he believed that God knew and that was sufficient. Likewise others will not always know why God acts in a particular way but they can be confident knowing, 'that in all things God works for the good of those who love him, who have been called according to his purpose' (Rom. 8:28). Everything depends upon God's achievements and the realisation of this fact teaches one to praise God. Always remember that God controls every situation and so you can be confident because you can say, 'My times are in your hands' (Psa. 31:15).

Seeing Jesus in the Scriptures

The parable of the Rich Fool told by Jesus (Luke 12:16–22) teaches that the man was foolish not because he was rich or successful but because he believed that he had no need of God. He failed to realise that it was impossible to control the calendar of his life. Likewise we cannot write in our diaries with certainty what we shall do tomorrow. We can prepare for the future, but we cannot plan it. It is God who changes our circumstances so that we shall be humbled or exalted.

'The day of the Lord will come like a thief in the night' (1 Thess. 5:2).

WEEK 4

The Rat Race

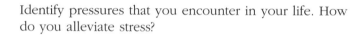

Opening Icebreaker

Identify pressures that you encounter in your life. How do you alleviate stress?

Bible Readings

- Ecclesiastes 4:4–8
- Matthew 6:25–34
- Philippians 4:11–13
- 1 Timothy 6:8

Opening Our Eyes

Certain representatives of the animal kingdom such as social insects are co-operative with each other. They manifest group integration and division of labour and so work as a team. Probably the most common examples are termites and various species of ants and bees. However, there are animals which do not co-operate and where individuals are so concerned about themselves that they will attack their own species. Such an animal is the rat. Hence, the words 'rat race' aptly describe the intensely competitive struggle to maintain one's position in work or life – a situation in which the law of the jungle prevails. Herbert Spencer and later Charles Darwin described it as the survival of the fittest.

Society today usually places emphasis upon speed and success regardless of the cost in human terms. Keeping up with the neighbours can be an extremely difficult and tiresome business. It's the rat race, and the primary motive for taking part is envy. Envy results in a person joining the race and addiction keeps them there because the more they have the more they want. Therefore, they have no enjoyment of their possessions.

No one can escape the accelerating pace of life. Yet each individual reacts differently. Some will achieve success while others cannot stand the pressure and give up or have a nervous breakdown. Psychological disturbance, physical disorders and spiritual depression increasingly affect the society in which we live and this despair may even lead to suicide.

An awareness of uncertainty within the world due primarily to terrorist attacks has made many people focus on the priorities of life. Often those in full-time jobs are increasingly searching to simplify their lives by reducing the mounting pressures that are encountered daily. Too many demands on time, excessive information and innumerable choices leave many feeling exhausted at the end of a day. It is not surprising that this is leading some to reassess their lifestyle. Is it to earn more, or is it to focus on family, relationships and other important values? A growing number of people are 'downshifting', that is to take a cut in salary in exchange for less responsibility, or to work fewer hours.

A minimalist form of living is also gaining in popularity. That is only to keep possessions which are absolutely essential for a comfortable existence. Throughout life one can accumulate numerous unnecessary items which are often a liability. Bookshelves may be laden with books that are never read. Are they necessary? A few helpful books thoroughly assimilated should suffice. Wardrobes may be filled with clothes that are never worn. Are they necessary? A clear-out of excessive baggage can be a useful first step towards attaining a more simplified and enjoyable lifestyle.

There are a few who have given up the rat race by adopting a carefree lifestyle and are proud to become dropouts. However, there is a danger that they lose their grasp of reality and their desire to achieve anything in life.

Ecclesiastes considers two extremes, which are both meaningless. Someone may achieve things in life by toil, though unfortunately the motivating force is rivalry and envy. Conversely, some adopt an attitude of laziness, which produces no worthwhile achievements. The answer to the problem lies between the two. 'Better one handful with tranquillity than two handfuls with toil and chasing after the wind' (Eccl. 4:6). This is a picture of someone who's content with what they've got.

Discussion Starters

1. When is ambition good?

2. When does ambition become sinful? Isn't a sinful way of life more exciting?

3. Selfish ambition results in competitive behaviour patterns; specify some of these.

4. Discuss the definition of envy. Give examples from the Bible of some who did dreadful things because of envy.

5. Think of some biblical characters who used power wisely and others who abused it.

6. Why do some people stay in the rat race when they no longer need to?

7. Read Ecclesiastes 4:9–12 and then discuss the importance of partnership.

8. What are some guidelines for successful teamwork?

Personal Application

The characteristics of a truly successful life will be co-operation instead of competition, contentment instead of covetousness and togetherness instead of loneliness. Anyone obsessed with wealth or self precludes all beneficial associations with others and so there will be no one to help in times of need.

If the witness of a church is to be effective its members must work together. Each member has received some spiritual gift designed not to serve the individual but the entire church.

Seeing Jesus in the Scriptures

Lasting contentment is never found in money or success but in Christ. The apostle Paul knew how to be content. He says, 'I have learned to be content whatever the circumstances. I know what it is to be in need, and I know what it is to have plenty … I can do everything through him who gives me strength' (Phil. 4:11–13). Contentment comes from knowing and doing the will of God and this enables one to remain calm in adversity and humble in prosperity.

WEEK 5

The Love of Money

Opening Icebreaker

Identify the most important things in life which money cannot buy. Love friendship Jesus

Bible Readings

- Ecclesiastes 5:10
- Ecclesiastes 5:15; see also Job 1:21
- 1 Timothy 6:10
- Matthew 6:24
- Hebrews 13:5
- Acts 5:1–10

Opening Our Eyes

Who is better off, the person with money or the person without? Usually people associate happiness with prosperity and misery with poverty. However, experience indicates that riches can never ensure lasting satisfaction. Paul Getty and Howard Hughes, both billionaires, died unhappy.

As useful as money is, it has limitations. Therefore, those who are wealthy are often failures, while those who are poor are masters at the art of living. The oil magnate and Baptist, John Rockefeller, said, 'The poorest man I know is the man who's got nothing but money.' True happiness bears no relationship to a person's bank balance and a sad fact of life is that some have great wealth without the ability to enjoy it. This is undoubtedly one of the most futile and frustrating experiences in life. Even worse than the addiction money brings is the emptiness it leaves. It's better to be stillborn than to have wealth and not be able to enjoy it (see Eccl. 6:3).

A disadvantage of wealth is that it can cause constant anxiety (Eccl. 5:12). All material possessions can be easily lost. Circumstances may change and a fortune can disappear overnight. Periods of boom and bust are a recurring feature of history.

Any financial investment is a risky business and there are frequent reminders that past performance is no guarantee of future prospects. Property prices can soar to create a housing boom, but they can also tumble and many have found themselves in positions of negative equity. Pension schemes can collapse and there are those who fear this possibility. These examples prove that wealth is unstable and therefore its retention uncertain. Whatever happens, people will certainly lose their wealth at death.

It must always be recognised that wealth is not our entitlement, it is God's gift (Eccl. 5:19). Remembering this basic fact enables one to be constantly thankful. There are many rich people who are not slaves to money. They enjoy it because they know that God gave it to them. Likewise they realise that it can be taken away at any time, but this does not affect their gratitude. They enjoy it today without the worry of losing it tomorrow. That is why Job, despite all his extreme difficulties could say, 'The LORD gave and the LORD has taken away; may the name of the LORD be praised' (Job 1:21). This is a sharp contrast to the reaction of his wife who said, 'Curse God and die!' (Job 2:9). The obvious difference in their attitude was that the wife never said the Lord gave and so she couldn't praise the Lord for taking it away. Job also reveals that for the Lord to withhold a gift or even take something away is not necessarily a sign of displeasure.

It is vital to keep your life free from the love of money because it is a root of all kinds of evil (1 Tim. 6:10). Even so, nowhere in the Bible does it say that one must be financially poor. The very wealthy Abraham (Gen. 13:2) was a friend of God (James 2:23); and the rich Joseph of Arimathea was a disciple of Jesus (Matt. 27:57). Many of God's people were and are extremely rich. It can be good to have money and to enjoy and share the things it can buy. But if you find there is some material thing that you can't live without then give it away. Undoubtedly your freedom depends upon it.

Discussion Starters

1. Money plays an important part in our everyday life and can influence one's character for better or worse. Think of some biblical examples of people who were corrupted by greed.

_____

_____

_____

_____

_____

2. Differentiate between having money and the love of money.

_____

_____

_____

_____

_____

3. Should one equate poverty with spirituality?

_____

_____

_____

_____

_____

4. It is impossible to be faithful to more than one master or ideal simultaneously. Discuss Matthew 6:24.

_____

_____

_____

_____

_____

5. Does prosperity indicate God's blessing?

_____

_____

_____

_____

_____

6. There are many who believe that if only they were rich they would be content. Is such an assumption true? Give examples to support your answer.

_____

_____

_____

_____

_____

7. Do you set your heart on more than you need and buy things which are unnecessary?

_____

_____

_____

_____

_____

8. We bring nothing into the world, and we can take nothing out of it. How should this influence our attitude to wealth?

_____

_____

_____

_____

_____

Personal Application

It is always important to remember that the real measure
of your wealth is how much you'd be worth if you
lost all your material possessions. If such things are the
dominant feature of your life then it's a waste of time
because ultimately they are meaningless. 'Do not store up
for yourselves treasures on earth, where moth and rust
destroy, and where thieves break in and steal. But store
up for yourselves treasures in heaven, where moth and
rust do not destroy, and where thieves do not break in
and steal' (Matt. 6:19–20). Earthly treasures are transient
while heavenly ones are moth-proof, rust-proof and
burglar-proof; that is, they endure for ever.

Seeing Jesus in the Scriptures

Jesus said a lot about money because it is so important.
There is a warning (Matt. 6:21) that where your treasure
is, there your heart will be also. This is well illustrated in
the story of the rich ruler who came to Jesus to ask what
he must do to inherit eternal life (Luke 18:18–30). Jesus
said to him, 'Sell everything you have and give to the
poor, and you will have treasure in heaven. Then come,
follow me' (v.22). This is not to say that everyone must
do the same thing. However, in this instance the man
loved earthly possessions and because of that it was the
necessary and only cure.

WEEK 6

Wisdom and Proverbs

Opening Icebreaker

'Look before you leap' and 'Chickens come home to roost' are well-known proverbs. Suggest some others that appear in everyday conversation. Do they offer wise advice? *Stitch in time saves nine*
Put the cart before the horse.

Bible Readings

- Ecclesiastes 7:11–12
- Proverbs 1:1–7
- Psalm 119:97–99
- 1 Kings 3:16–28
- James 3:13–18

Opening Our Eyes

The writer of Ecclesiastes, having considered the subject of wealth, turns to wisdom and concludes that it is better to be wise than wealthy (Eccl. 7:11–12). 'Blessed is the man who finds wisdom, the man who gains understanding, for she is more profitable than silver and yields better returns than gold. She is more precious than rubies; nothing you desire can compare with her' (Prov. 3:13–15).

True wisdom is much more than knowledge; it is spiritual insight obtained only by supernatural revelation. Wisdom necessitates having insight to reach correct conclusions. This is well illustrated in the proverb, 'Foresight is better than hindsight, but insight is best.' Wisdom is to know the will of God and so it is supreme (Prov. 4:5–7). Hence, getting wisdom is the most important thing you can do! Because true wisdom is a supernatural gift it can only be obtained by asking God through prayer.

Although wisdom is greater than knowledge it is also important to study so as to be well qualified to deal with life's many challenges. A thorough education is important and people should endeavour to utilise the abilities God has given them. However, it should be remembered that education can often prove to be totally inadequate to deal with many problems. Numerous examples throughout history confirm that knowledgable people are not necessarily wise.

Thankfully one is never confronted with the problem of choosing between knowledge and wisdom but, like Solomon, can say to God, 'Give me wisdom and knowledge' (2 Chron. 1:10). And, 'God gave Solomon wisdom and very great insight, and a breadth of understanding as measureless as the sand on the seashore' (1 Kings 4:29). Solomon communicated much of his wisdom in proverbs and songs. 'He spoke three thousand proverbs and his songs numbered a thousand and five' (1 Kings 4:32). The book of Proverbs and the Song of Songs are examples of his writings. In Ecclesiastes 7 the writer introduces a number of proverbs in which two groups are compared to show that one is better than the other. These contain wise advice, which should be heeded and practised for if you only quote them they are of no use. The poet John Keats, in a letter to George and Georgiana Keats, wrote, 'Nothing ever becomes real till it is experienced – even a proverb is no proverb to you till your life has illustrated it.'

Examination of the proverbs in Ecclesiastes raises the question of whether or not they have anything in common. Although it's perhaps not immediately obvious, the answer is 'Yes'. They all clearly indicate that a wise person is living for the future rather than the present. For instance, 'A good name is better than fine perfume.' Why? It is because the fragrance of the perfume lasts for only a few hours while a good name will last you a lifetime. The wise person is someone who thinks long term whereas the fool lives only for the here and now. It can be likened to the Esau syndrome. Esau, unlike his brother Jacob, lived only for the present and paid the penalty (Gen. 25:29–34).

Our immediate reaction to this would probably and rightly be to consider Esau extremely foolish. But how many people today live only for the present? How many people believe that it is better to buy now and pay later? How many people are exchanging eternal glory for something trivial? What fools to have such a short-term outlook.

Discussion Starters

1. What is wisdom and how does it differ from knowledge?

_____

_____

_____

_____

2. The fear of the Lord is the beginning of wisdom (Psa. 111:10; Prov. 1:7; 9:10; 15:33). What do you understand by this?

_____

_____

_____

_____

3. Compare the characteristics of counterfeit and genuine wisdom (James 3:13–18).

_____

_____

_____

_____

4. A major concern repeatedly expressed throughout the Bible is that of godless religion. What type of worship is unacceptable to God?

_____

_____

_____

_____

5. What are the main dangers associated with godless religion?

_____

_____

_____

_____

_____

6. Why should the day of death be better than the day of birth?

_____

_____

_____

_____

_____

7. Why is it better to go to a house of mourning than to a house of feasting?

_____

_____

_____

_____

_____

8. Do you look to the future, live only for the present, or dwell in the past?

_____

_____

_____

_____

_____

Personal Application

A wise person lives for the future rather than the present, but even worse is to live in the past (Eccl. 7:10). Sometimes people talk about the good old days, but things can appear better with the progress of time than they actually were. In reality one age is very much like another. 'What has been will be again, what has been done will be done again; there is nothing new under the sun' (Eccl. 1:9).

The wisdom to be found in the proverbs is timeless in its application. Therefore, it is wise to benefit by yesterday's experiences; but to be over-concerned by past failures or content with past successes will arrest future progress. Don't live in the past but look to the future and look to God.

Seeing Jesus in the Scriptures

It is important to note that the Bible never associates wisdom with the unbeliever. Hence, one's first experience of wisdom comes with conversion. Wisdom, righteousness, holiness and redemption can only be found in Jesus (1 Cor. 1:30). Wisdom is found first at the cross and then it develops by studying God's infallible Word. Paul writing to Timothy says, 'From infancy you have known the holy Scriptures, which are able to make you wise for salvation through faith in Christ Jesus' (2 Tim. 3:15).

WEEK 7

Concluding Thoughts

Opening Icebreaker

Read together Isaiah 53.

Bible Readings

- Ecclesiastes 12:13–14
- Exodus 20:1–18
- John 13:34
- Romans 2:1–16

Opening Our Eyes

So far all the paths tried in the search for satisfaction have failed. They always will, because whatever you try has been done before. However, this is not the main theme of Ecclesiastes. It is not a confession of failure or disillusionment. Neither is the message sceptical or pessimistic. Rather it is an inspired work that directs one to God who alone can satisfy our deepest needs. Clearly the conclusion is to 'Fear God and keep his commandments.' This is true wisdom.

Old and New Testament authors repeatedly state that God is a God of love; this is not a fluctuating emotion but a constant characteristic. Even so, it must be realised that this is one attribute of God among many and so should not be given undue emphasis. The mistake so many make is in supposing that the grace and the law of God are irreconcilable opposites. It is easy to consider a part of the Bible in isolation and so miss the truth.

To obtain a balance it must be remembered that God is also a God of holiness and therefore a God of wrath. He is intolerant of sin. The prophet Habakkuk acknowledged this by crying out to God, 'Your eyes are too pure to look on evil; you cannot tolerate wrong' (Hab. 1:13). Therefore, how can a God of holiness allow anyone to heaven?

There is a great danger in placing undue emphasis upon a particular attribute of God because you will inevitably reach the wrong conclusion. It would appear plausible that because God is a God of love He could never send anyone to hell. Consequently there are some who after a lifetime of sin have no fear of God.

At the other extreme are those who fear God's wrath, also because of misunderstanding. They think of God only as a stern judge making a note of everything anyone does ready for the Day of Judgment. For many years Martin Luther, who played such an important part in the Protestant Reformation, was plagued by a feeling of overwhelming guilt and terrorised by the thought of a vengeful Deity until he experienced the loving forgiveness of God through Jesus Christ.

The wrath of God is not a loss of self-control by God, but it is His utter detestation of sin, which He will certainly punish. The true fear of God is that of reverent awe, which results from faith and it will be shown by keeping His commandments.

The sovereign God makes laws for His kingdom and this as been so from the beginning (Gen. 2:16–17). When God brought His people out of Egypt He gave them laws – the Ten Commandments (Exod. 20:1–18). Obeying God's law is the duty of all people and to disobey reveals that there is no fear of God or His judgment.

Is God just or merciful? Will He punish or pardon sin? 'The wages of sin is death, but the gift of God is eternal life in Christ Jesus our Lord' (Rom. 6:23). Consequently, the answer is that He can do both, and if that appears to be a contradiction to anyone it is because they have never been to the cross. It is there that the law and the love, the justice and the mercy of God operate together. The penalty of sin is paid by Christ Who is innocent, so that we who are guilty are acquitted. There is no other way that leads to life.

Discussion Starters

1. The writer of Ecclesiastes repeatedly uses the phrase, 'under the sun'. Discuss the significance of this.

2. Do you believe that life on earth is a preparation for something greater and eternal, or is it meaningless?

3. What are the dangers of placing undue emphasis upon a particular attribute of God?

4. Discuss what you understand by 'the wrath of God'.

5. How would you answer someone who claimed that God is too kind to condemn anyone?

_____
_____
_____
_____
_____

6. Why was the cross of Christ necessary?

_____
_____
_____
_____
_____

7. Is it true that to enjoy life in its fullest sense, there must ultimately be a sense of purpose?

_____
_____
_____
_____
_____

8. Now all has been heard. What is your conclusion? Is life meaningless or meaningful?

_____
_____
_____
_____
_____

Personal Application

If you do not believe in an afterlife, the obvious conclusion, whatever your achievements, must be that ultimately everything in life is meaningless. A chasing after the wind. The clear message of Ecclesiastes is that you can never find the true meaning of life until you find God and keep His commandments. This is the greatest fact of life.

> Fear God and keep his commandments,
>   for this is the whole duty of man.
> For God will bring every deed into judgment,
>   including every hidden thing,
>   whether it is good or evil.

(Eccl. 12:13–14)

Seeing Jesus in the Scriptures

Jesus came that we may have life, and have it to the full (John 10:10), and it is available to whosoever believes in Him (John 3:16). May God make you one of them!

The following forcefully sums up the final answer to the cry of 'Meaningless!' 'When the perishable has been clothed with the imperishable, and the mortal with immortality, then the saying that is written will come true: "Death has been swallowed up in victory" ... Therefore, my dear brothers, stand firm. Let nothing move you. Always give yourselves fully to the work of the Lord, because you know that your labour in the Lord is not in vain' (1 Cor. 15:54,58).

Leader's Notes

Week 1: Getting Nowhere

Opening Icebreaker
The idea of this exercise is to create a relaxed atmosphere by encouraging the group to talk about their life and what they would change if they could.

Aim of the Session
To show that if you confine your thinking to 'under the sun', it will become impossible to answer the major questions relating to the purpose of life.

Discussion Starters
1. It is essential to be able to accurately watch and interpret things as they occur. Never over-emphasise or minimise any aspect of your search because a balanced view is essential when searching for the truth. Hence, preconceived opinions must always be avoided. Also avoid the tendency to accept what others say without examination. Be like the Bereans who examined the Scriptures every day to see if what Paul said was true (Acts 17:11). Finally answer all questions honestly so that your search for satisfaction will leave you with a sense of achievement.

2. Consider the advantages that are gained from a lifetime of hard labour. The aim is not to discourage one from being industrious, or to say that no advantage can be gained from work. But this question affirms that it is impossible to show any real purpose or profit gained, if there is nothing beyond this life. 'What good is it for a man to gain the whole world, yet forfeit his soul?' (Mark 8:36).

3. Life for many can appear to be weary and tiresome. Therefore, consider the importance of breaking a regular routine. God commands us to observe times of physical and spiritual refreshment (Exod. 20:8–11). Discuss whether or not it is important to keep Sunday special.

4. The aim is not to look at the problems and pressures of life but rather to consider expectations. Should one be a pessimist or an optimist in relation to the future? In answering this question there is a prior assertion that needs to be made: one ought to be a realist. It would be foolish not to face up to possibilities however awful they may be. What are these possibilities?

5. Going to work each morning, returning at night, watching television and then going to bed can make one question the purpose of life. Even those with action-packed lives can sometimes wonder where it's leading. This particularly applies to the middle-aged who might feel that they have achieved nothing and see no prospects for the future. Stress that it is vital to have a sense of purpose or life will be meaningless.

6. You are looking for things like appetite, challenge, envy, greed, pride, showing off, etc. Consequently some are buying things they don't want, with money they don't have, to impress people they don't like. Consider the influence of advertising and its extravagant claims to change our lives for the better.

7. Surely there is occasionally something that can be called new? Obviously there are changes for better or worse and it would be foolish to deny the inventiveness of humankind. However, there is a monotonous sameness about human activity and experience which shows that there is nothing new

under the sun. Human nature remains the same in every generation and country.

8. What is happiness? Can you be happy during times of difficulty? Paul wrote, 'Our light and momentary troubles are achieving for us an eternal glory that far outweighs them all' (2 Cor. 4:17). Looking to the future, and the glory which awaits all Christians, keeps things in perspective.

Week 2: The Search for Satisfaction

Opening Icebreaker
This should produce some imaginative discussion and reveal different aspirations within the group.

Aim of the Session
A tour of exploration that attempts to discover the purpose of life.

1. The German-born psychoanalyst and author, Erich Fromm, said, 'Greed is a bottomless pit which exhausts a person in an endless effort to satisfy the need without ever reaching satisfaction.' This competitive attitude will inevitably result in casualties. Explore the daily pressures of life and how they influence society. Jesus relieves our burdens and gives us rest (Matt. 11:28–30).

2. You're looking here to stress that no material possession can ever provide ultimate satisfaction. No matter how much you see, you are never satisfied. No matter how much you hear, you are not content (Eccl. 1:8–11). Only God can meet your deepest needs.

3. True riches do not consist of material things and so a godly person is not primarily interested in amassing a vast amount of possessions. Rather, contentment comes from knowing and doing the will of God and this enables one to remain calm in adversity and humble in prosperity. It is more blessed to give than to receive (Acts 20:35).

4. Knowledge can be used for good or evil and so instruction in religious and moral principles is essential. God's Word is a source of wisdom and insight. It is relevant to every situation and will thoroughly equip one for every good work (2 Tim. 3:16–17). The psalmist says, 'Your word is a lamp to my feet and a light for my path' (Psa. 119:105).

5. The main benefit of education is not the acquisition of facts, but learning how to use them to advantage. Otherwise they serve no purpose.

6. The idea of this exercise is to make the group members think seriously about their future. It's very easy to go through life and avoid asking vital questions. Only a fool lives for the here and now while a wise person thinks long term.

7. Knowing the presence of God in one's life brings peace and joy even in difficult times (Hab. 3:17–18). Anyone who does not trust God can never be fully satisfied.

8. There are those who, through lack of wisdom, in their search for satisfaction become addicted to various vices and need help. One needs to pray for such people and offer practical assistance. The first thing for any addict is to accept that a problem exists, for often they practise self-deceit and do not realise their sad state. To acknowledge powerlessness and unmanageability for any form of addiction is the first step towards

recovery. An Ethiopian proverb says, 'He who conceals his disease cannot expect to be cured.' Also remember that professional help will probably be necessary, for friends may not be competent to counsel all of the problems.

Week 3: A Time for Everything

Opening Icebreaker
This can cover a wide range of discussion. Consider how scientific discovery can change the world for better or worse. Discuss the benefits of humanitarian aid and the atrocities of terrorist activities. The greatest event that changed the world was the death and resurrection of Jesus.

Aim of the Session
To explore the preciousness of time and its use.

1. Jews who returned from Babylon to their homeland intended to rebuild the Temple but very soon said, 'The time has not yet come for the LORD's house to be built' (Hag. 1:2). They concentrated on building their own houses, something of which they could be proud, while the house of the Lord was still only a foundation, which could be built later when they had more time. It's an attempt to establish a truce between conscience and covetousness, but they are deceiving themselves just as we can deceive ourselves.

2. 'Yes, I am interested. Yes, I should like to help. Unfortunately it's not possible at present because I'm too busy doing other things.' Remember that all Christians should work hard at whatever they do

(2 Thess. 3:6–13). Usually it is the busiest people who are willing to do more.

3. All of us have the same amount of time at our disposal, 24 hours in every day. How do we use it? Things that probably matter to us are our education, our work, our home and family, our hobbies, etc. Christians must also devote time to their Christian life and make the most of every opportunity.

4. It is easy for Christians to become distracted by trivialities. This is well illustrated by the two sisters, Martha and Mary, who both loved Jesus (Luke 10:38–42). Mary is sitting eagerly listening to what Jesus had to say while Martha concerns herself about all the work that needs to be done. She is distracted by things that were not at that moment important. The mistake made by Martha should be a warning to us all. Studying God's Word and prayer can so easily be neglected in the hectic lifestyle encountered by so many today.

5. Don't do tomorrow what can be done today, for tomorrow might never come. Think of missed opportunities and remember that time is a gift from God which should not be wasted. 'Now is the time of God's favour, now is the day of salvation' (2 Cor. 6:2). A time will come when it is too late.

6. During times of difficulty it is tempting to think that God is not fair. But rest assured that ultimately God's justice will prevail. God has appointed a day in which He will judge the world. Judgment and punishment are promised for all sin.

7. It would be foolish and sinful to try and precisely predict the date when Christ will return. Instead people should be alert and use their time profitably. The watchful person will be dressed ready for service

and keep their lamps burning (Luke 12:35). A servant should always be loyal to their master, even if it's inconvenient.

8. Life, like money, should be productive and so one should use it to the fullest possible advantage. The parable of the talents (Matt. 25:14–30) emphasises the duty of work. Repeatedly warnings are given against laziness, for example, Ecclesiastes 10:18. Time is a precious gift of God and so should be used wisely. One day God will bring every deed into judgment (Eccl. 12:14).

Week 4: The Rat Race

Opening Icebreaker
The idea of this exercise is for the group to identify the pressures that they encounter and provide an opportunity to talk about how stress can be alleviated.

Aim of the Session
To show that an extremely competitive attitude, or dropping out from society, serve no useful purpose.

1. It is good to aim for a position of power, provided that the motive is correct. People should aim to be successful in their career not for their own benefit, but that it will help others and glorify God. Paul's great ambition was to preach about Christ (Rom. 15:20).

2. Ambition becomes sinful when it is not used to glorify God. It can become the dominant feature of one's life and be used by Satan to lead one to destruction (Matt. 4:8–10). Selfish ambition can also affect friendships by creating unhealthy competitiveness (Mark 10:35–45).

Those who think that the sinful way of life is more exciting should read Luke 15:11–32. The pleasures of wild living always eventually result in suffering.

3. Ambition for power can affect people in many ways. They may strive for personal position or glorification or they may want to prevent someone else from occupying such a position. To achieve their aim some will pay almost any price in terms of time, effort, money, moral standards and violence. Their ultimate goal will be personal gain at the expense of others. The writer of Ecclesiastes (4:13–16) shows the futility of selfish ambition.

4. Our English word 'envy' comes from the Latin *in video* meaning 'to look against'; that is, to look with grudging displeasure at someone because of what they are or have. Biblical examples you could look at are: the murder of Abel, Joseph thrown into the pit, Saul pursuing David and the 'elder brother' (in the parable of the lost son). Jesus was brought before Pilate because of envy (Matt. 27:18).

5. Biblical examples you could look at of those who were wise are Solomon (1 Kings 3:5–14); and Daniel, Hananiah, Mishael and Azariah (Dan. 1:17–20). Examples of those who abused power, and did evil in the sight of the Lord, are the series of kings who followed Solomon. This cycle was completed by Ahab who was worse than any of those before him (1 Kings 16:30). He was a weak man in a position of power.

6. Staying in a position of power and maintaining a high standard is extremely difficult. The Russian-born American composer, Irving Berlin, said, 'The toughest thing about success is that you've got to keep on being a success.' It's tough at the top and sadly some,

because of addiction, tenaciously try to stay there well beyond their period of usefulness.

7. Consider the practical benefits of working together both from the individual and group point of view. Individuals in times of trouble often isolate themselves and so it's difficult for anyone to help. Not only do they suffer, but also the Church, which is sometimes likened to a human body with many parts (1 Cor. 12:12–31). Each part performs a specific task and contributes to the working of the entire body. Without this the life of the Church will suffer. Sadly in some situations a few members appear to do all the work while others, except for attending Sunday worship when convenient, are idle. Every member of the Body of Christ should realise their responsibility and employ and develop their various gifts.

8. Read 1 Corinthians 13:1–13. Inspired by the Holy Spirit, Paul gives us a love letter which can uncover our weaknesses and challenge us to grow in faith. Without love, one's work will always be formalistic or fanatical.

Week 5: The Love of Money

Opening Icebreaker
Money cannot buy you love, respect, personality, guaranteed health, salvation, immortality, or many of the things that make life worth living.

Aim of the Session
The futility of living only for the acquisition of riches.

1. Judas Iscariot betrayed Jesus for 30 pieces of silver (Matt. 26:14–15); Gehazi (2 Kings 5:20–27) and Ananias and Sapphira (Acts 5:1–10) told lies because of money.

2. 'The love of money is a root of all kinds of evil' (1 Tim. 6:10). Observe that it is not money which is the problem but the love of it. The desire for riches has frequently been the cause of lies, perversions of justice, exploitation of the weak, robberies, frauds, murders and wars. Those who love money never have enough and so they are miserable. Greed and contentment are opposites.

3. Spirituality should not be equated with poverty or wealth. Paul said, 'I know what it is to be in need, and I know what it is to have plenty' (Phil. 4:12). God's blessing cannot be measured on the scale of material assets.

4. Covetous people are never content and misers are always miserable because their addiction results in them becoming a slave to possessions. Those who fail to achieve mastery over money will certainly find that it gains mastery over them. Jesus said, 'No-one can serve two masters. Either he will hate the one and love the other, or he will be devoted to the one and despise the other. You cannot serve both God and Money' (Matt. 6:24). It is impossible to be faithful to more than one master or ideal simultaneously.

5. A heresy today is the prosperity gospel, which claims to make you healthier and wealthier. It implies that poverty or suffering indicates a failure to claim God's promises. This is what some want to believe, but nowhere does the Bible make such claims. Quite the contrary (2 Tim. 3:12).

6. There are those who try to find happiness in material possessions. They believe that if they were rich all their troubles would quickly vanish. Consequently the aim is to earn more on every possible occasion. Money can be like a drug in that the more you have the more you want, and the more you get does not result in satisfaction. Jay Gould, the nineteenth-century American financier, who died unlamented worth some $100 million, is claimed to have said on his deathbed, 'I'm the most miserable devil in the world.'

7. Get the group to discuss how they react to temptation. Do they buy things which are unnecessary? What do they think about a minimalist form of living? Do they keep things which are only gathering dust? Contentment begins when one realises that there is more to life than our time on earth. Then everything takes on a new value.

8. I'm reminded of two people who were talking about a person who had just died. One enquired, 'How much did he leave?' and the other replied, 'Everything.' 'Naked a man comes from his mother's womb, and as he comes, so he departs. He takes nothing from his labour that he can carry in his hand' (Eccl. 5:15, see also Job 1:21). We bring nothing into the world and we can take nothing out of it (1 Tim. 6:7). Therefore, it's foolish to worship something that you cannot keep. Our true riches are in heaven, where Christ is (Matt. 6:21).

Week 6: Wisdom and Proverbs

Opening Icebreaker

The idea of this exercise is to show that a proverb contains a general truth that can easily be remembered. Usually they offer wise advice.

Aim of the Session

To show the value of wisdom, and that it can be ours when we seek its source, God. It's not what we know, but *who* we know.

1. True wisdom is spiritual insight and therefore greater than knowledge. The English writer and clergyman, Charles Caleb Colton, drew attention to this: 'It is better to have wisdom without learning, than to have learning without wisdom; just as it is better to be rich without being the possessor of a mine, than to be a possessor of a mine without being rich.'

2. Emphasise that 'fear' is best understood as 'reverent obedience'. Obedience to God reveals that our judgment is sound. Only fools despise wisdom and discipline.

3. Ungodly wisdom can be recognised by signs of bitter envy, selfish ambition and boasting. 'Do not be wise in your own eyes' (Prov. 3:7). The characteristics of true wisdom are listed in James 3:17. Observe that purity is placed before peace. If the maintenance of peace involves an unacceptable moral compromise, then peace must be abandoned. Lord John Russell rightly said, 'If peace cannot be maintained with honour, it is no longer peace.' Peace at any price is not what the Bible teaches.

4. There are many instances within the Bible where God was not worshipped as He should be. For example, Joel 2:12–13. Rending their garments but not their hearts reveals that their religion had become an outward show rather than an inward reality. Consider the unacceptable worship of the Pharisees (Matt. 16:6) and the letter to the church at Ephesus (Rev. 2:1–7). A simple definition of godless religion is, 'that which doesn't meet God when it comes to worship'.

5. Godless religion is fatal because those who practise it are deluded into believing they are right with God when they are not. There are those who regularly meet with a church over a period of many years who do not know Jesus Christ as their Lord and Saviour. They attend out of a sense of patronage rather than privilege. Never assume acceptability by God because of works (Eph. 2:8–9). The only thing that anyone can contribute to their salvation is the sin from which they are saved. Only by appealing to God's mercy can forgiveness be attained.

6. To suggest that the day of death is better than the day of birth can at first appear strange and some in the group might question its validity. Certainly most of us are happy to think about our birthday, but there is a reluctance to talk about our death day. This is a mistake, for one of the greatest facts of life is death. The day of death has more to teach us than the day of birth. It is the destiny of us all and so we should take this to heart.

7. Funerals are better than feasts and sorrow is better for you than laughter. Hence, the heart of the wise man is in the house of mourning. His thoughts relating to life, death and judgment will be serious while the fool will think of nothing but merriment and laughter. Death and its consequences will be an unmentionable subject in the company of fools.

8. Discuss the dangers of living in the past or only for the present. Consider the concept of life after death. Is this life on earth a pilgrimage leading to glory?

Week 7: Concluding Thoughts

Opening Icebreaker

Isaiah 53 deals with purpose and achievement. From shameful suffering and inhumane treatment emerge triumph and glory. Invite group members to comment.

Aim of the Session

The tour of exploration is now complete and all has been heard. What is your conclusion?

1. To work within the framework under the sun and limit yourself in time will result in disappointment. This is because one's view will be restricted to that which can be seen in our observable world. It is to draw a line between earthly and heavenly realities and ignore all spiritual values. Consequently such a confinement will lead to the conclusion that everything in life is meaningless.

2. To look above the sun and beyond the grave to the glory which is to come will reveal what life is all about. This is well illustrated in the incident where Stephen was stoned to death (Acts 7:55–56). It can be achieved only by divine revelation.

3. Ask the group how biased reporting in newspapers and on television can influence one's opinion. Emphasise the importance of basing decisions upon facts and not feelings. Read 2 Timothy 3:16 and observe the word

'all'. A thorough knowledge of the Bible enables one to keep a right attitude toward God and others.

4. The wrath of God describes holy intolerance of sin. Habakkuk acknowledged this by crying out to God, 'Your eyes are too pure to look on evil; you cannot tolerate wrong' (Hab. 1:13). Paul calls this punishment 'the coming wrath' (1 Thess. 1:10) and refers to its time of execution as 'the day of God's wrath' (Rom. 2:5). One day the full power of God's anger will be seen (Rev. 6:16–17).

5. Martyn Lloyd-Jones (*Atonement and Justification (Romans 3:20 – 4:25)*, 1970, Banner of Truth, p.74) states that in the Old Testament there are more than 20 words to describe the wrath of God and these words are used in their various forms a total of 580 times. Only by rejecting this overwhelming evidence can anyone deny the awful reality of the wrath of God.

6. Draw out the facts that:
   - We are all sinners (Rom. 3:23).
   - God's punishment of sin is death, but the gift of God is eternal life in Christ Jesus our Lord (Rom. 6:23).
   - Assurance of this (Rom. 10:13).
   - There is no other way (John 14:6).

7. Ascertain what the major aim in life is of each group member. Will it give ultimate satisfaction? Then discuss how discovering God's purpose begins by seeking His forgiveness. Read Romans 12:1–2 and see how Paul's great purpose in life was to win others to Christ. There is a clear command to all believers to proclaim the gospel message (Matt. 28:19–20).

8. Although the Bible reveals the future it does not answer every question. Even so, there is sufficient to give one hope and confidence. The Christian looks

forward to the return of the Lord Jesus Christ. He who suffered our temptations and yet never sinned will return to judge and punish or reward accordingly. Without the final judgment, life would be meaningless for it is obvious that many wicked people prosper in this life while the righteous suffer. However, justice will ultimately prevail (Eccl. 12:14).

National Distributors

UK: (and countries not listed below)
CWR, Waverley Abbey House, Waverley Lane, Farnham, Surrey GU9 8EP.
Tel: (01252) 784700 Outside UK (44) 1252 784700

AUSTRALIA: KI Entertainment, Unit 31 317-321 Woodpark Road, Smithfield, New South Wales 2164. Tel: 02 9604 3600 Fax: 02 9604 3699

CANADA: David C Cook Distribution Canada, PO Box 98, 55 Woodslee Avenue, Paris, Ontario N3L 3E5. Tel: 1800 263 2664

GHANA: Challenge Enterprises of Ghana, PO Box 5723, Accra.
Tel: (021) 222437/223249 Fax: (021) 226227

HONG KONG: Cross Communications Ltd, 1/F, 562A Nathan Road, Kowloon.
Tel: 2780 1188 Fax: 2770 6229

INDIA: Crystal Communications, 10-3-18/4/1, East Marredpalli, Secunderabad – 500026, Andhra Pradesh. Tel/Fax: (040) 27737145

KENYA: Keswick Books and Gifts Ltd, PO Box 10242-00400, Nairobi.
Tel: (254) 20 312639/3870125

MALAYSIA: Salvation Book Centre (M) Sdn Bhd, 23 Jalan SS 2/64, 47300 Petaling Jaya, Selangor. Tel: (03) 78766411/78766797 Fax: (03) 78757066/78756360

Canaanland, No. 25 Jalan PJU 1A/41B, NZX Commercial Centre, Ara Jaya, 47301 Petaling Jaya, Selangor. Tel: (03) 7885 0540/1/2 Fax: (03) 7885 0545

NIGERIA: FBFM, Helen Baugh House, 96 St Finbarr's College Road, Akoka, Lagos.
Tel: (01) 7747429/4700218/825775/827264

PHILIPPINES: OMF Literature Inc, 776 Boni Avenue, Mandaluyong City.
Tel: (02) 531 2183 Fax: (02) 531 1960

SINGAPORE: Alby Commercial Enterprises Pte Ltd, 95 Kallang Avenue #04-00, AIS Industrial Building, 339420. Tel: (65) 629 27238 Fax: (65) 629 27235

SOUTH AFRICA: Struik Christian Books, 80 MacKenzie Street, PO Box 1144, Cape Town 8000. Tel: (021) 462 4360 Fax: (021) 461 3612

SRI LANKA: Christombu Publications (Pvt) Ltd, Bartleet House, 65 Braybrooke Place, Colombo 2. Tel: (9411) 2421073/2447665

USA: David C Cook Distribution Canada, PO Box 98, 55 Woodslee Avenue, Paris, Ontario N3L 3E5, Canada. Tel: 1800 263 2664

For email addresses, visit the CWR website: www.cwr.org.uk
CWR is a Registered Charity – Number 294387
CWR is a Limited Company registered in England – Registration Number 1990308

Day and Residential Courses
Counselling Training
Leadership Development
Biblical Study Courses
Regional Seminars
Ministry to Women
Daily Devotionals
Books and Videos
Conference Centre

Trusted all Over the World

CWR HAS GAINED A WORLDWIDE
reputation as a centre of excellence for
Bible-based training and resources. From
our headquarters at Waverley Abbey
House, Farnham, England, we have
been serving God's people for over 40
years with a vision to help apply God's
Word to everyday life and relationships.
The daily devotional *Every Day with
Jesus* is read by nearly a million people
in more than 150 countries, and our
unique courses in biblical studies and
pastoral care are respected all over the
world. Waverley Abbey House provides a
conference centre in a tranquil setting.

For free brochures on our seminars
and courses, conference facilities, or
a catalogue of CWR resources, please
contact us at the following address.
**CWR, Waverley Abbey House, Waverley
Lane, Farnham, Surrey GU9 8EP, UK**

Telephone: **+44 (0)1252 784700**
Email: **mail@cwr.org.uk**
Website: **www.cwr.org.uk**

CWR Applying God's Word
to everyday life and relationships

Our *Cover to Cover* resources enable you to dig deep into God's transforming Word

Be inspired by Esther's heroic courage

The book of Esther is a piece of history that has it all: an orphaned girl from an ethnic minority becomes an empire's most powerful woman.

From this seven-session Bible study you will gain inspiration and insights as you enter the rich 'pantomime' that is the story of Esther.

ISBN: 978-1-85345-511-7
£3.99

Walk the 'holiness highway'

Like today's world, Isaiah's time was marred by moral decadence, political corruption, injustice and idolatry.

With this seven-session Bible study, you will discover how you can live above it all and effectively play your part in God's plan for the renewal of creation.

ISBN: 978-1-85345-510-0
£3.99

Also available in the *Cover to Cover Bible Study* series

1 Corinthians
Growing a Spirit-filled church
ISBN: 978-1-85345-374-8

1 Timothy
Healthy churches – effective Christians
ISBN: 978-1-85345-291-8

23rd Psalm
The Lord is my shepherd
ISBN: 978-1-85345-449-3

2 Timothy and Titus
Vital Christianity
ISBN: 978-1-85345-338-0

Ecclesiastes
Hard questions and spiritual answers
ISBN: 978-1-85345-371-7

Ephesians
Claiming your inheritance
ISBN: 978-1-85345-229-1

Esther
For such a time as this
ISBN: 978-1-85345-511-7

Fruit of the Spirit
Growing more like Jesus
ISBN: 978-1-85345-375-5

Genesis 1–11
Foundations of reality
ISBN: 978-1-85345-404-2

God's Rescue Plan
Finding God's fingerprints on human history
ISBN: 978-1-85345-294-9

£3.99 each (plus p&p)

Price correct at time of printing

Cover to Cover Every Day
Gain deeper knowledge of the Bible

Our *Cover to Cover Every Day* bimonthly dated notes will take you deep into each book of the Bible over a five-year period.

Each issue features contributions from two different authors and a reflection on a psalm each weekend by Philip Greenslade.

- Covers every book of the Bible in a rolling five-year curriculum
- Daily Scripture readings and a suggested prayer
- Highly respected and well known authors

ISSN: 1744-0114
Only £2.49 each (plus p&p)
£13.80 for annual UK subscription (6 issues)
£13.80 for annual email subscription
(available from www.cwr.org.uk/store)

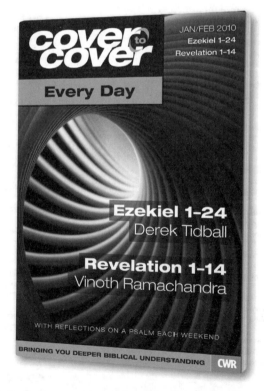